# ABOVE AUCKLAND

First published in 2003 by New Holland Publishers (NZ) Ltd
Auckland • Sydney • London • Cape Town

218 Lake Road, Northcote, Auckland, New Zealand
14 Aquatic Drive, Frenchs Forest, NSW 2086, Australia
86–88 Edgware Road, London W2 2EA, United Kingdom
80 McKenzie Street, Cape Town 8001, South Africa

www.newhollandpublishers.co.nz

ISBN: 1 86966 042 0

Publishing manager: Renée Lang
Design: Dexter Fry
Editor: Pat Field

A catalogue record for this book is available from the
National Library of New Zealand

10 9 8 7 6 5 4 3 2 1

Colour reproduction by Microdot, Auckland, New Zealand
Printed in China through Colorcraft Ltd, Hong Kong

# ABOVE AUCKLAND

PHOTOGRAPHS BY DAVID WALL

TEXT BY DON DONOVAN

# FOREWORD

AUCKLAND: the City of Sails, of course . . . and of boats and beaches and marinas and hills, all situated on a fertile isthmus between two stunningly beautiful harbours. We Aucklanders know all about that.

It's also a city of houses and high rises, highways and traffic, congestion and people – lots of people in lots of houses. It's a big city nowadays. Living in a big city can make a person quite myopic. Each of us has our own special territory; patches that we are familiar with and feel comfortable in. We have individual travelling routes to and from home and work; and our own ways of getting in and out – and across the metropolis.

During the course of our everyday lives we usually look at the structures in our city from just one angle, which tends to be either from street level or from our workplace windows. We feel disoriented, however, when we try to identify roads and locations from the Sky Tower viewing platform because we are seeing what should be familiar from a novel perspective.

This book of spectacular aerial photographs, *Above Auckland*, gives me something of that same feeling – a twist of the familiar; a fresh look at the place I have lived in for nearly the whole of my life and thought I knew so well. Auckland is a collection of different places; different life-styles. There are many new 'Aucklands' here seen from another viewpoint, making me ponder on how little we really know of the piece of New Zealand we like to claim as our own.

The stunning photography in *Above Auckland*, complemented by an entertaining text of historical and descriptive snapshots, presents an image of a vibrant, confidently established city – still young, still growing, still making mistakes. Still a great place to live.

Dame Catherine Tizard

# INTRODUCTION

FOR THOUSANDS OF YEARS black-backed gulls have effortlessly glided from the Hauraki Gulf to the shores of the Tasman Sea, looking down upon a land map seen by human eyes only in the last century. With the advent of popular flight came the privilege of being able to see the shape of Auckland and to appreciate the beguiling untidiness of its harbours and bays, river estuaries, volcanoes, forests and peninsulas, and the reckless splatter of its inshore islands. An untidiness that adds up to the magic of what is now the 'City of Sails'.

While the land form has changed little in those years – apart from the one emergent volcano, Rangitoto, and a few minor intrusions and reclamations – the imprint of the human hand has vastly changed its surface. Since it was identified, little more than 150 years ago, as the site of a future city, the population of its greater area has grown to accommodate well over one million people of ever widening ethnic diversity. With that expansion have come changes of land usage in the service of its citizens: at the outskirts, farms that supply dairy, meat and crop products; closer in, smallholdings and market gardens; in the suburbs, housing, shopping malls, schools, factories; and in the central business district, the glittering glass towers that distinguish all modern cities.

Its post-Maori origins were born out of Victorian England when the first Governor of New Zealand, William Hobson, a Royal Navy man with an eye for a deep-water port, selected the area surrounding Waitemata Harbour for settlement. With compelling loyalty to the 'old country' the streets, wharfs and parks of the city were given names such as Victoria, Albert, Princes, Queen, Wellesley, Waterloo, Nelson and Hobson (of course). The settlement grew first around the southern shores of the entrance to the Waitemata and then filled out to the south-east and west to border the more extensive, but less useful, southern harbour, the Manukau. Some early development of the peninsula that forms the north shore of the Waitemata took place at Devonport but it wasn't until 1959, when the Auckland Harbour Bridge was built, that any significant northern expansion took place.

The region that is Auckland is comprised of four distinct cities: Auckland, Waitakere, North Shore and Manukau; and three outlying districts, Rodney, Franklin and Papakura. It's probably true to say that most of the people who live in those areas call themselves Aucklanders when identifying their geographies; and it's certain that anybody from outside lumps them all together as they would New Yorkers, Londoners, Sydneysiders or Tokyoites. Around 30% of New Zealand's people live here yet the region comprises only 2% of the country's land area. Of all the new migrants to this country, 70% of them settle in Auckland; hence its ethnic diversity and its increasingly cosmopolitan nature.

From the air it's apparent that Auckland spreads as a low-level city; none of its downtown buildings could be called skyscrapers, most of its houses are single-storeyed bungalows, self-contained on small gardens. Only 13% of its citizens live in high-rise or multi-unit dwellings but it is expected that as the city grows and space becomes scarcer one-third will be in higher-density accommodation by 2050 by which time Auckland's urban area will have expanded by 5000 hectares or 10%.

It's probable, though, that when a bird's eye-view of Auckland is published fifty years from now nothing short of another Rangitotoan volcanic catastrophe will present the black-backed gull with an unfamiliar landscape; any differences from the superb images David Wall presents to us in *Above Auckland* will be superficial.

(Above) Rangitoto Island.

(Page 1) Auckland CBD with Princes Wharf in the foreground.

(Pages 2–3) Auckland's Sky Tower.

(Page 4) Looking towards the city from Coxs Bay.

(Page 6) Looking over Takapuna and Lake Pupuke.

(Overleaf) Downtown Auckland City at night.

The city's most prominent architectural feature is the Sky Tower; it has become something of a symbol of Auckland's civic status, being the tallest tower in the southern hemisphere. (It is higher than Sydney's AMP Tower, and it tops Paris's Eiffel Tower by a large margin.) Sky Tower is 328 metres high, was finished in 1997 and took thirty-two months to build. It can be seen from a great distance and stands as a navigation marker – if you can see the tower you can easily find your way downtown.

The extent of Auckland's surrounds can be appreciated from Sky Tower's main observation deck. In this view (right) the low cone of Rangitoto Island looms beyond Devonport peninsula and the inner-city wharfs.

While it's an act of faith – especially for the faint-hearted – to stand on the glass floor of the observation deck (below right) and take a perpendicular peep at the ground below, it's quite safe; the glass slabs are 38 mm thick and concrete-strong. For those of a bolder nature not content with glass floor gazing, Sky Jump (opposite) will set the pulses racing. It's a thrilling, controlled plunge of 192 metres at a speed of 60 km/h from level 53 of the tower. Unlike bungy in which one falls head first, Sky Jump uses a harness attached to a cable so that the jumper skims like Superman, birdlike, to the ground.

The next adventure beyond Sky Jump is 'Vertigo', a climb inside the telecommunications mast to 300 metres. If you want to be any higher above Auckland than that you'll have to take a helicopter!

From the touch-screen kiosks on its main observation deck Sky Tower's 'Eye in the Sky', linked to external cameras, allows viewers to select and closely examine specific parts of surrounding Auckland. They can see live images such as those of the motorway lanes that flow like neon snakes into and out of the city, passing under Hopetoun Street and Karangahape Road (above). Closer in is the absolute heart of the city where Victoria and Wellesley Streets cross Queen Street. Dominant at that crossing (left) are triangular twin buildings, one named for Phillips Fox, the other the National Bank Centre. They and their high-rise neighbours represent some of New Zealand's most valuable real estate and house major local and international commercial and professional organisations. The Crowne Plaza Hotel is on Albert Street while the dark area at the top of the picture is Albert Park.

(Overleaf) Auckland's main thoroughfare, Queen Street, slices through the central business district on its way south from Queen Elizabeth II Square.

As Auckland grew it became necessary to infill and modify the natural shoreline and to extend quays to accommodate more ships; but later, special container facilities elsewhere made it possible for some of the wharfs to take on a new life by becoming imaginative extensions of the downtown city. Princes Wharf (opposite page and left), virtually a continuation of Hobson Street, is not only the overseas terminal but also carries the five star Hilton Hotel (beside the moored ship), luxury apartments, shops, offices and parking for 1000 cars. Farther east (above) the ferry berth and Queen's Wharf are the terminus for the ferries that ply across Auckland Harbour. The 'Edwardian baroque' Ferry Building, of sandstone and brick, was built in 1912 on reclaimed land.

Just how closely downtown Auckland city is connected to the Waitemata Harbour and the Hauraki Gulf is shown in the view (left) that includes all of the city wharfs from the Viaduct Harbour in the foreground to the container complex at Mechanics Bay. In the distance are Hobson Bay and, beyond, the eastern residential suburbs.

The Viaduct Harbour (above), once almost entirely given over to fishing vessels, has undergone continuous change and development, most recently to accommodate competitors in the international Louis Vuitton and America's Cup regattas. Today, with the America's Cup Village, it is a haven for ocean-going cruisers, pleasure boats, and some remaining vessels of the old fishing fleet.

From across the South Pacific or by way of the Tasman Sea a constant stream of container ships services the import and export needs of a country which is perhaps the most isolated of 'Western economy' nations in the world. One such ship (right) heads purposefully towards the container terminals that lie closest to the entrance to the Waitemata Harbour, a complex of modern facilities that have largely replaced the cargo handling of the earlier city wharfs.

Pre-packing of cargo into standard cubical modules – containers (below left) – replaced the laborious and labour-intensive business of ship loading in the final decades of the twentieth century. It was probably the most radical change in freight handling since Phoenician times and demanded completely different systems and facilities. The Axis Intermodal container port, in close and convenient proximity to the commercial centre of the city (left), was started in the early 1970s and has continued to expand and modernise since. The Axis Fergusson Container Terminal (in the foreground) is the largest of the wharfs, and is currently undergoing a 35% enlargement. It has four quayside cranes and twenty-five straddle carriers; its 600 metres of berthage can accommodate three medium-size ships or two large (the largest refrigerated container ships in the world come into Auckland). It provides the principal area for temporary storage and marshalling of containers. Beyond the triangular Freyberg Wharf and its neighbouring Jellicoe Wharf is the Axis Bledisloe Container Terminal, somewhat smaller than the Axis Fergusson but nevertheless New Zealand's second-largest container port.

Over 560 000 standard containers a year pass through this complex and their contents amount to 65% of New Zealand's imports by sea and 27% of exports. The Port of Auckland trades with 160 ports and 73 countries, operates 24 hours a day, seven days a week and employs over 480 staff.

New Zealand has far more than its fair share of world-class yachties, highly experienced and capable, from the smallest one-crew dinghy sailors to solo round-the-worlders. It's hardly surprising that many of them come from Auckland whose bays abound with boat harbours full of keelers and cruisers owned by local people. The best known of the marinas is Westhaven (opposite page and above); it nestles below the southern motorway off-ramp of the Harbour Bridge within minutes of the city centre.

Many young yachties make their start as crew on the family boat; while others learn the ropes on the *Spirit of New Zealand* (left), a steel-hulled barquentine operated by the Auckland-based Spirit of Adventure Trust Board.

Albert Park (above), characterised by its
pink paths, neat lawns, flower beds, and
a variety of shade trees was, in the middle
of the nineteenth century, the site of Albert
Barracks, the only piece of which remains
is a wall with loopholes in the Auckland
University complex adjacent, across Princes
Street. It is the nearest formal park to the
city centre (bottom left in the main
illustration), the steps of its steep north-
western edge being no more than three
minutes' walk from Queen Street.

A peaceful haven, it is much frequented by
students and office workers, a pleasant
place to chat and stroll or take lunch
alfresco on a summer's day.

The roofs of inner Auckland, especially those of the older areas that lie outside the central business district, are much of a patchwork of different ages, varied colours and materials, and a spectrum of conditions from new and smart to rusty neglect! Ponsonby (opposite above) is one of the oldest residential suburbs and boasts some of the best of colonial domestic architecture – substantial, well-built kauri cottages many of which, rescued from decay, have been lovingly restored and maintained. Ponsonby Road bisects the suburb and is noted for its superb restaurants, street-side cafés and boutique shops. Karangahape Road (opposite below) is of similar character. It provides a link from Auckland city centre to the Ponsonby Ridge and Great North Road and in doing so bridges the northern feeder lanes of the motorway. 'K' Road, as it's colloquially known, with a uniquely cosmopolitan life of its own, is also a busy shopping street but in a state of constant change and improvement as big-city redevelopment encroaches; despite which it still clings to its Victorian beginnings.

Through the heart of a city whose streets were first conceived for horse-drawn traffic a motorway system bravely attempts to facilitate access and egress to and from the north, north-west and the south. At its most convoluted and serpentine it has earned the title 'Spaghetti Junction' (left) and heaven help anybody who takes the wrong exit!

However much the city might expand and evolve, the 163-hectare Auckland Domain (left) will always be the emerald in its crown. Enclosed within the dense forest of specimen trees that separates the Domain from Parnell and Grafton, its swelling greenness is a leisure ground for the people of Auckland, a family park for picnicking, kite flying, organised cricket and informal Samoan kilikiti, and summer concerts that often attract over 200 000 visitors. The Auckland War Memorial Museum (above), opened in 1929, is at the Domain's centre, Pukekawa Hill. Among other exhibits it has the largest collection of Maori artefacts in the world.

The Domain Wintergarden (below) is particularly famed for its fernery, and the elegant twin glasshouses display a huge range of tropical and subtropical plants.

Although hedged in by later additions, the old High Court building in Waterloo Quadrant (above) has an air of nineteenth-century refinement. Particularly fascinating are its gargoyles and sculpted heads of dignitaries carved by German immigrant Anton Teutenberg.

Auckland's home of cricket and rugby union football, Eden Park (left), is hallowed ground. It was laid out in 1900, became the home of Auckland cricket in 1910 and rugby in 1925. The stadium can hold 50 000 spectators and is likely to be full when international rugby matches are played, or when the home team or regional Auckland Blues compete in the national provincial championships. When night games are played the park glows with passion – like the crater of an active volcano!

What started life in 1905 as the city's rubbish destructor complete with a 38-metre-high chimney is now Victoria Park Market. Now transformed into a shopping complex of stalls, kiosks, booths and cafés it nevertheless retains the cobbles-and-bricks character of its beginnings.

Only from the air can one appreciate just how much generous greenness is added to the landscape by raceways and the formal garden areas that often surround them.

Alexandra Park (above), adjacent to Cornwall Park and once intriguingly known as 'Potter's Paddock', is the head-quarters of the Auckland Trotting Club which was formed in 1890. Its banked, shimmering silvery-pink track, 1021 metres in circumference, is an aggregate of oyster shell and gravel.

The Auckland Racing Club was founded in 1874. Its Ellerslie Racecourse (left), beside the southern motorway, stages 26 race meetings a year including some of New Zealand's principal thoroughbred racing events such as the Auckland Cup, Easter Handicap and the New Zealand Derby. It also doubles as a function and convention centre. Its 12 hectares of grounds, with magnificent gardens and conference facilities, attract visitors to occasions far removed from racing; such events as car shows, antiques fairs, wine festivals and art exhibitions.

The old Arts Building of the University of Auckland (above) is younger than its decorative Gothic architectural style suggests. Finished in 1926 to the design of American architect Roy Alstan Lippincott, it was once the centre of the university but has rather become an architectural symbol as additions have been made to the campus.

From 1888 girls shared a boys' grammar school in the city but it was administered as separate-gender schools and great efforts were made to keep the sexes apart; the girls had a separate entrance, and a 3-metre-high wall divided the playground! Wisely, in 1906 a decision was made to separate them completely and so the Auckland Girls' Grammar School was created. The severe and institutional building (right) that stands next to Auckland's oldest park, Western Park, has been its home in Howe Street since 1909.

In the context of local architecture Auckland Grammar School (left), distinguished by its lavish cupola-topped towers and curlicued gables, is astonishing. It is completely unlike anything else in the city. Its style is 'Spanish Mission', common in California. It was completed in 1916 to the design of architects Charles Arnold and Richard Abbott and has maintained a reputation for academic excellence throughout its history.

A different sort of education is handed out in the grim confines of Mount Eden Prison (above) and many infamous New Zealanders have passed through its stark cells. Prisoners built it of a loveless bluestone in the 1880s to the fanciful design of a Mr Burrows of the Public Works Department. Outdated and impractical, it is nevertheless an Auckland landmark.

(Overleaf) Maungakiekie (One Tree Hill) and Cornwall Park.

Dominion Road (opposite) is one of the longest straight stretches of suburban thoroughfare in New Zealand. It runs almost north to south, starting at Newton near Karangahape Road. On its way to Mt Roskill, which overlooks the northern shores of Auckland's western Manukau Harbour, it passes along a ribbon of 'villages' each with its own set of shops and offices. The old residential area of Mt Eden (left) typifies the traditional Aucklander's desire to have a snug home and garden in a quiet street which might, typically, have a patch of neat lawn, a rose bed and the odd plaster gnome or flamingo. Farther east at Remuera (below) stately homes with pools and tennis courts tell of a more affluent life-style.

From 1877 until early in the twentieth century Auckland's water supply came principally from Western Springs (above). The pump house and its machinery can still be seen at the Museum of Transport and Technology (MOTAT) which is one of the many attractions of what is now a huge park and playground. The grounds also feature a sports and entertainment stadium where, among other events, speedway racing and pop concerts are staged. The largest permanent attraction at 'The Springs' is the internationally esteemed Auckland Zoological Garden (left). The zoo (which connects to MOTAT by vintage tramway) was opened in the 1920s and is home to the country's biggest collection of native and exotic animals. A large aviary exhibits many of New Zealand's native birds – some extremely rare – and in addition to the usual hippos, monkeys, lions and giraffes there are a rain forest, and a mini-zoo of rural New Zealand creatures called Tui Farm, especially presented for children.

Before the Auckland Harbour Bridge was built the journey to North Shore could be done only by ferry or by an arduous drive around the top of the Waitemata Harbour. The completion of the bridge injected life and vitality into Devonport, Takapuna, the East Coast Bays and farther, greatly boosting the population of those new city suburbs. The four-laned bridge, wryly known as 'The Coat Hanger', was British-built in 1959 to leap just over a kilometre from Erin Point on the city side to Stokes Point. It soon became inadequate and in 1969 two new lanes were added to each side of the main structure by a Japanese company, thus the 'Coat Hanger' gained 'Nippon Clip-ons'! Traffic count is over 160 000 vehicles a day and growing, giving rise to speculation as to when an alternative bridge, or even a tunnel, might be added.

Just west of the harbour bridge at Birkenhead is the dolls'-house-pink Chelsea Sugar refinery (left) established in 1884 to win a bounty offered by a government anxious to process sugar locally instead of importing it from Australia. It's a bizarre complex, the original part built of a million bricks hand-made from the clay of its site excavation. These days the New Zealand Sugar Company's Chelsea brand is in every household's pantry.

Below the bridge, on the Devonport Peninsula, two promontories reach out towards the main city. The first is Bayswater (above) whose 400-berth marina, begun in 1994, has added 4 hectares of reclaimed land to Bayswater Point. Stanley Point (opposite) juts west from Devonport and from its tip you can look across the harbour up the length of Queen Street.

Volcanic North Head (left) protects the attractive suburbs of Devonport and Cheltenham Beach that lie close against its western slopes. It was topped by Fort Cautley and three artillery batteries in 1886 because – incredibly in the light of history – it was feared that Russia might attack New Zealand! A romantic history has been woven around the hill's internal maze of tunnels; nobody seems to know their extent or what military equipment might be stored in them: speculation includes a complete seaplane! North Head is now a reserve but has retained one of the old 'disappearing guns' (below) as a memorial. A Royal New Zealand Navy base still operates west of Devonport at Stanley Bay (above).

(Overleaf) Lake Pupuke, Takapuna.

Beautiful beaches grace the whole length
of the North Shore. The best known is
Takapuna Beach (above) which, on a
summer's day, is popular with family
swimmers, boaters, picnickers and
sun-bathers. In a more general view (right)
Takapuna lies at the far left. It is separated
from the grand sweep of Milford Beach,
in the centre of the photograph, by tiny
Thorne Bay. In the foreground, tucked
inside Rahopara Point and its historic
reserve, is Castor Bay (once known as
Castor Oil Bay). Lake Pupuke, beyond
Milford, is a volcanic crater. Maori
mythology has it that Rangitoto Island
rested there before relocating to the
Hauraki Gulf.

(Overleaf) Campbells Bay and Red Bluff.

Enclaves of the North Shore such as Devonport and Takapuna were, from early times, served by the passenger and vehicular ferries that plied Waitemata Harbour. Consequently, although road access was less than ideal, those suburbs grew and had a life of their own, self-sustaining and independent of the city.

But until the harbour bridge was built in 1959 the farther north one went the more sparsely populated were the bays and beaches. Holiday cottages and 'baches' (simple cabins whose name derives from bachelor) – often built of the crudest and simplest of materials – dotted the bays. They were, typically, used at weekends and holidays by Auckland city folk who would load their cars with cooking pots, portable radios, seaside comforts and camping gear and trundle away on a long run on a rough, narrow road around the top of the Waitemata Harbour to their inexpensive paradises.

From 1959 the 'baches' were steadily replaced by permanent dwellings, some of which, today, are sumptuous in the extreme; land values soared and prime positions on cliff top or beach side became much sought after. Roads were upgraded; schools, shops and commercial and professional services became established, and development spread farther inland, filling what had been farmland. Now North Shore is a city in its own right and magnificence has come to what were once remote destinations such as Murrays Bay (above left), Torbay and Waiake Beach (far left) and Browns Bay (left).

Long Bay (left and above) is at the top end of the east coast bays of the North Shore. As such it is the least residentially developed. A regional park, it is devoted to public enjoyment and recreation with grassy picnic areas behind a safe swimming beach; a short-stay caravan park; a children's playground with its own miniature train; and coastal walks through native bush and farmland. Views from its cliffs, of the Hauraki Gulf and the Whangaparaoa Peninsula to its north are impressive. Maori, who had occupied the district since before the fifteenth century, called it Oneroa – long beach. It was sold by them to the Crown in 1854 after which the Vaughan family – whose house is still there – bought it and remained in possession of the land until the mid-1960s when it was purchased by the Auckland Regional Authority.

The more modern domestic suburbs make an interesting contrast with those of the early twentieth century. Unlike Mt Eden (page 39) today's planned subdivisions, of which Massey (above) is a good example, prove the growth in affluence and expectation of the average Aucklander. The roads are wider, the houses are larger, every one has a garage, many double; and inside there will be a treasury of home appliances and entertainment centres such as earlier Mt Edenites might never have dreamed of!

An even newer suburb, built on farmlands and strawberry fields around a nineteenth-century village, is Albany (opposite), site of the Oteha Rohe campus of Massey University and the new North Harbour Stadium (left), a minor masterpiece of engineering gracefulness.

A small fleet of yachts moors stem to stern in the Weiti River (above), which drains into Okura Bay at the southern neck of the Whangaparaoa Peninsula. Tidal and river currents often make mooring tricky and are known to provoke colourful 'boatie' language at times. The peninsula, which thrusts about 16 kilometres eastwards into the Hauraki Gulf, has become considerably built up in recent years; along its length charming headlands, coves, and bays like Little Manly (opposite left foreground) have attracted increasing numbers of residents many of whom are willing to commute daily to Auckland city. Beyond Little Manly are Matakatia Bay and Gulf Harbour. On the northern side is Waiau Bay, and Little Barrier Island seen here lying partly below the far horizon.

Like a dream Gulf Harbour (opposite) appeared almost overnight out of nothing, but, of course, in reality it took a little longer than that. It lies on the southern side of Whangaparaoa Peninsula, with 18 000 square kilometres of Hauraki Gulf on its doorstep. Built around a natural haven formerly called Hobbs Bay, it started with the marina, finished in 1988, which claims to be one of the largest in Australasia with 969 berths and space for 25 'super-yachts'.

Inland from the marina there's a small, canal-side village of luxury apartments with individual boat docks. It has its own shops, restaurants and a small hotel, and its architectural style, unusual for New Zealand, would perhaps more closely resemble the condominiums of southern California. The village is just a champagne cork's throw from the Gulf Harbour Country Club among whose 'memorable experiences' are billiards, tennis and squash courts, a swimming pool, gymnasium, bar and restaurant. And then there's the golf course, 18 holes designed by world-renowned golf architect Robert Trent Jones Jnr. From its cliffside holes and fairways (left) many a golfer might be distracted by the fabulous views across the Gulf.

The nearby Whangaparaoa Military Camp (left below) is even more exclusive than the country club but it's probable that the warriors who serve there don't consider it so.

North of the Whangaparaoa Peninsula is Orewa (left) on the Hibiscus Coast. At one time it was no more than a resort into which flooded holidaymakers who swelled its camping and caravan parks for, perhaps, four weeks of the year, and then disappeared. The caravan and camping parks are now subsumed in a thriving town, at the end of the latest extension of the northern motorway from Auckland city. With more than 6000 residents and a growth rate of four times the national average, it's a town especially loved by youthful older people retired to space and sunshine. Orewa's beach is 3 kilometres of glorious sand and never looks crowded even on the sunniest holiday of the year. The Orewa River enters Whangaparaoa Bay by way of its picturesque estuary at the southern end of the beach (below). Across the river are the tiny Rosano Park and the cliffs and gentle sands of Red Beach.

No doubt the engineering is highly professional but from the air the apparent recklessness with which houses have been built on the cliffs at the north end of Orewa Beach is breathtaking – as are the views from any one of them (above). Behind the houses, State Highway 1 – which will become a quieter coast road when the northern motorway extensions are finished – winds towards Hatfields Beach (right), a short-run jewel of sand and shell with pohutukawa trees for shade. At Hatfields, as it's commonly known, Sir Robert Muldoon, a former prime minister, had his weekend 'bach', a simple affair where he could forget state and walk barefoot with his mates. In the forested hills beyond the beach is the next best thing to heaven – a retirement home.

Wai = water, wera = hot; the ancient Maori knew a good thing when they found it and were so possessive of their thermal springs, which they called Te Rata (the doctor) that they set up fortified pa (stockades) to defend them from attacking tribes. Despite that, in 1844 a Scotsman, Robert Graham, managed to get title to some of the hot springs that bubble from natural fissures on the beach side and set up a spa with a hotel and bath houses. Waiwera resort (right), north of Hatfields, gained quite a reputation for therapy among Aucklanders who would come by steamer ferry (infinitely preferable to the early roads) to take the healing waters. They still come to the mineral pools and spa cubicles where water temperatures range from 28 to 44 degrees celsius; they bring their families, and they come to stay in the hotel, attend conferences, dine out, take beach and bush walks, take whirling rides and water slides (above) and even buy specially bottled local water from a resort the extent of which would make Robert Graham and the early Maori boggle.

(Overleaf) Wenderholme Regional Park between the Waiwera and Puhoi River mouths.

Four kilometres from the end of Whangaparaoa Peninsula lies the low, forested island of Tiritiri Matangi (above and right). Its Maori name acknowledges the prevailing north-east winds that blow towards it from Great and Little Barrier Islands. Farming stripped most of its 220 hectares of native bush but it is now a reserve and protected by the Department of Conservation for its wildlife, scientific and recreational values. More than half of the island is now forest again; the remainder is kept as grassland where rare species of birds such as the takahe, a flightless rail that was only just saved from extinction, may thrive unmolested by predators.

Above its south-eastern cliffs is an historic lighthouse. Built in 1864, it's one of the oldest in New Zealand. It was prefabricated of cast iron in England and brought here in sections for assembly on its site. It's over 21 metres high, flashes every fifteen seconds and since 1990 has been solar powered.

Waiheke is the largest island in the Hauraki Gulf, home to about 8000 permanent residents. High-speed, reliable ferry services have turned the island into a suburb of Auckland and many of the people who spend their days in city offices spend their nights and weekends on Waiheke Island. Its name means 'ebbing water' in Maori. The Ngati Maru tribe first settled there in the tenth century but the island was much fought over for the following thousand years. Today, what was once an island of kauri forest is given over to vineyards, olive groves and pasture. Expanding settlements, mainly in the west, cluster around the beaches and headlands of bays such as Oneroa, on the northern side of an isthmus shared with Blackpool (opposite), the deeply sheltered Putaki Bay and Ostend (above) and Matiatia Bay (left) at the western end of the island, the main arrival point for the ferries from Auckland. The new terminal at Matiatia will look after the needs of an increasing number of visitors and residents.

On 13 August 1840 William Brown bought the volcanic island of Motukorea (above) from the local Maori owners, renamed it for himself, and took up residence there with John Logan Campbell, who would later become known as 'the father of Auckland' for his property developments and benefactions. It's claimed that they were Auckland's first permanent residents. After Brown came a plague of rabbits; today the island is a bare bump of browning grasses with a few trees for decoration.

Contrasting with Brown Island's baldness is bush-covered, 260-metre-high Rangitoto (left). A geological newcomer to the Hauraki Gulf it's the youngest and largest of Auckland's volcanoes, having erupted from the sea about 700 years ago. Since then, on the meanest of topsoils and under the harshest conditions a low pohutukawa-canopied forest has grown; some of its 200 species of flora, many of them with their roots embedded in other plants, are unique.

(Overleaf) Okahu Bay, Orakei Jetty and Tamaki Drive.

A knob of land that commands impressive views across the entrance to the Waitemata Harbour to North Head and Rangitoto Island, Bastion Point once sported a battery of guns installed to meet a threatened Russian invasion of 1873 – a newspaper hoax of impressive outcome! More artillery was installed during the Second World War. Two of the gun emplacements remain incorporated in the expansive memorial mausoleum, built on the point, to Michael Joseph Savage (above), New Zealand's first Labour prime minister from 1935 to 1940. East of the point, Mission Bay (right) is one of a series of north-facing, sun-trap beaches, among the most desirable of domestic and holiday suburbs and no more than 15 minutes from downtown Auckland. The old Melanesian Mission House (far right) from which the bay gets its name was built in 1860 and is now a restaurant.

(Overleaf) St. Heliers and Achilles Point with Browns Island beyond.

In 1840 Governor William Hobson decided that the future capital of New Zealand should be somewhere on the isthmus that separates the Waitemata and Manukau Harbours. Accordingly, from his short-term capital in Russell, Northland, he sent his colonial Surveyor-General Felton Mathew to pinpoint exactly where Auckland would make its start. Felton Mathew considered a site at what is now Hobsonville, at the top end of the Waitemata Harbour, but soon rejected it as too shallow. In the end he recommended a spot where Panmure now stands, on the Tamaki River (left above). But naval captain Hobson perceived that despite its breadth the river could not compare with the deep waters of the lower Waitemata so he overruled his surveyor with the consequence that the present Auckland city, whose streets were laid out by Felton Mathew, became the capital until 1865.

Access from the sea was all important in that early, virtually roadless land and it's likely that even in their wildest dreams neither Hobson nor Felton Mathew could have imagined an Auckland laced with tarmac freeways and roads, lined with houses to accommodate hundreds of thousands of people, serving an isthmian sprawl that would, in time, absorb and sur-round Panmure and the adjacent suburbs to its east, west and south. In many ways, although Hobson's choice was right, Felton Mathew's recommendation is vindicated, especially considering Panmure's growth as evidenced in the six highways that meet at its central roundabout (left) and, close by, a small part of the grounds of one of New Zealand's largest automotive dealers (opposite left) whose offering of cars is so extensive that customers are conveyed in golf carts to inspect them.

The seductive fairways of the Pakuranga Country Club Golf Course (right) add a patch of green relief in among the clustered houses of Highland Park and Botany Downs. Farther west, across Pakuranga Heights, on the shores of the Tamaki River the 4.2-hectare grounds of St Kentigern's College (above) promise that schooldays will be happy days. 'Saint Kent's' was established in 1953 to educate Presbyterian boys; 50 years of changing times saw girls admitted as pupils for the first time in 2003. Very much in the forefront of modern education, the college claims that every student has a personal notebook computer and that 98% of its pupils qualify for tertiary study.

Tucked into the eastern shore of the Tamaki estuary, Half Moon Bay Marina (opposite) has berths for 500 keelers and cruisers. The photograph shows the moorings full and the car parks empty but at weekends and holidays it's the other way around when the marine-minded dwellers of east Auckland take their recreation exploring the islands of the Hauraki Gulf. The smaller marina and adjacent building is the headquarters of the 4000-member Bucklands Beach Yacht Club. When it was formed in 1949 its first 'clubhouse' was a 3 x 2 metre wooden box that was kept behind the local post office and carried to the beach on Saturdays! The new clubhouse was started in 1981 and the 100-berth marina added in 1988. Beyond the yacht club marina is a terminal for ferries to and from Auckland city, and a car ferry that services Waiheke Island.

Those fortunate enough to own a boat but not to have a marina berth brave the caprices of the tide and weather at less sheltered moorings in the Tamaki River estuary, or moor their boats parallel to the sands of Bucklands Beach (left). Question: how do the boaties get to their boats? Answer: by dinghy or breast stroke!

(Overleaf) The peninsula of Bucklands Beach and Eastern Beach.

Past Bucklands Beach is Howick Golf Course and, on what was the site of Te Waiarohia fortified pa, the memorial to Captain Edwin Musick (opposite), the pilot of the first commercial Pan Am flying boat into Auckland in 1937. He died a year later in a mid-air explosion near Samoa. More memories are preserved at the historic Howick Colonial Village (above) where relocated houses, a courthouse and church recreate, from the period 1840-1880, a settlement of Fencibles – British army pensioners. The cosseted rinks of the Howick Bowling Club (left) look almost like green solar panels in the summer sun.

In 1841 the population of metropolitan Auckland was 2895. By 1901 it was 67 226. One hundred years later it had grown to almost 1.2 million. Little wonder then that the region has metamorphosed into an aggregation of cities and boroughs, that its roading system fights a continual battle to keep up and that the demand for living space has pushed urban areas farther and farther into the country.

While there was always a small village at Howick it was encircled by farmlands until new arrivals to New Zealand's fastest grow- ing and largest city took up sections on proliferating residential subdivisions such as Botany Downs (opposite), south of Howick. It's a community which appeared almost out of nothing; fresh, unblemished, full of hope and promise, and fully serviced with enormous shopping malls, an eight-screen cinema complex, parks, schools, and health services including a well-thought-of and much used maternity unit.

The grander, if only slightly older, houses of Mellons Bay (above right) and Cockle Bay (below right), south-east of the Bucklands Beach peninsula, command fabulous views of Tamaki Strait and Waiheke Island.

New Zealand has an enviable reputation for thoroughbred horses – some say they're the best – and the country's largest sales centre is at the handsome complex of New Zealand Bloodstock Limited at Karaka, near Papakura, beside the southern motorway (left). It was built in 1987 on 20 hectares of land, its stable sheds have 700 holding boxes, and in the polygonal building at its heart some 3000 thoroughbreds are sold at a number of auctions every year to buyers from all over the world. To the east, Drury Creek slides under the southern motorway between Runciman and Drury (opposite) and weaves its lazy, tidal way seaward to join the Manukau Harbour by way of Pahurehure Inlet. Like all of the scores of small streams in this area the creek drains rolling lowlands well cultivated into farms of dairy and beef cattle, cropping and market gardens. It was a much disputed area in the 1860s when Maori uprisings that had started in Taranaki spread north through the Waikato and even threatened the youthful Auckland city, and many a farmer and his family would, at the end of the working day, take overnight refuge in a military redoubt for fear of attack. The political aftershocks of a compromise peace still rumble into the twenty-first century.

Unlike the course at suburban Pakuranga (page 87), Pukekohe Golf Course (above) has room to breathe, its 6000 square metres of manicured greens and tree-lined fairways being surrounded by undulating farmlands, as is the flourishing town from which it gets its name.

Pukekohe (right) which, in Maori, means 'the hill where the kohekohe tree grows' is a town built on highly productive soil. As with Drury and all the early settlements in this district, relationships with Maori played a large part. The New Zealand government bought the Pukekohe Block from the local tribe in 1843 but so richly did the settlers profit from its fertility that the previous owners protested. Wisely, the government renegotiated the deal: Maori were happy, settlers were happy and the township was spared the miseries of the 1860s battles that bedevilled other parts of the district.

The main activity of the Pukekohe district is market gardening, and probably the first images that enter an Aucklander's mind when Pukekohe is mentioned are those of vegetables: potatoes and onions mostly. But many other crops grow here: cabbages, cauliflowers, lettuce, carrots, brassica, broccoli, pumpkins and even kiwifruit. The aerial photograph, full of the tertiary shades of an artist's palette, emphasizes the richness of Pukekohe's soil. Basically clay loam, its burnt sienna hue comes from volcanic deposits, gifts of ancient eruptions from the cones of Auckland, resulting in some of New Zealand's most fertile soils. The yellow fields in the foreground are mustard; at maturity the crop will be ploughed into the earth to enrich it by conversion into humus.

One of the delights of the southerly flight path into Auckland International Airport on the Manukau Harbour is the sudden arrival into view of the surrounding lush green farm fields (above). Particularly glorious on a late summer afternoon, they welcome the newcomer and hearten the returning traveller. It's an airport in a rural landscape and yet no more than 30 minutes by road from downtown Auckland. As the aircraft descends glimpses might be caught of the meandering headwaters of the harbour (right) where they are fed by the Waimahia Creek. Either side of the stream mangroves flourish – indications of a healthy ecosystem. In the middle-distance is Wattle Downs; Manukau Golf Course, the southern motorway and Takanini lie beyond.

Auckland's two great harbours come closest at a narrow neck of land that has Green Bay and Blockhouse Bay (left) at its south and Avondale and Waterview on the northern side. Pushing deeper into the Waitemata is the old-established suburb of Point Chevalier (opposite) with its beach-side Harbour View Reserve and the pretty Coyle Park at its tip. The park was named after Barney Coyle, one-time mayor of Mt Albert. At the base of Point Chevalier the north-western motorway carves between Western Springs and Chamberlain Park Golf Course towards the Te Atatu Peninsula (above).

A turning off the north-western motorway leads to the intimate village of Titirangi (right) which, in Maori, means 'long streaks of cloud in the sky'. It nestles among trees overlooking the middle reaches of Manukau Harbour. It's a place much favoured by artists and writers and many of its houses, often built upon poles on steep hillsides, evidence impressive creativity both in their design and engineering.

From Titirangi's winding main street a scenic drive traverses the ridge of the vast Centennial Memorial Park, and Waitakere Ranges Regional Park which, among tracts of superb native forest, contains many of the reservoirs from which Auckland city receives its water supplies.

Access roads also run from Titirangi down towards Wood Bay (opposite) and the hamlets that dot the northern shores of the harbour's entrance: Laingholm, Parau, Cornwallis, Little Huia and Whatipu at the end of the road where the land stops and the Tasman Sea begins.

Perhaps the greatest contrast between the Manukau and Waitemata Harbours is the behaviour of the sea. The Waitemata is sheltered and relatively tranquil but the Manukau opens to the Tasman Sea and its relentless drive from the west. Although a kindliness lies within, and the cultivated bays of Huia and Little Huia promise peace (far left, below) the prospect of negotiating the Manukau bar at its entrance (above left) would daunt the heart of the toughest old sailor. It was on this bar in 1863 that New Zealand's worst sea disaster occurred when HMS *Orpheus*, a 21-gun corvette powered by steam and sail, ran aground on its middle bank; of a complement of 259 officers and men 189 crew died. Bits of the ship are still being found and a memorial is erected on tiny Paratutae Island near Whatipu.

Outside the harbour, heading north up the Waitakere coast is Karekare beach, between two cliff escarpments (below left). Families come here to picnic at the foot of the Karekare Falls, for the more adventurous there's rock-scrambling, parapenting, surfing and swimming; and every year the sands drum to the hooves of horses in the Karekare beach races.

The waters of Kitekite Falls (left) drop by three silver threads from the dense Waitakere bush to feed the Glen Esk and Piha streams, ultimately to find their way into the Tasman Sea through the black sands of Piha beach (opposite). It's the most popular of all the west coast surf beaches, drawing many weekend and holiday visitors, and home to others fortunate enough to have baches or more substantial dwelling houses. The beach is divided by the impressive and aptly named Lion Rock on top of which is the site of an ancient Maori pa. The rock is destination for an annual bagpiped Anzac Day parade when homage is paid to those who died at war. It's a dramatic beach on a powerful coast beset by hidden dangers, that's why it has an active, much called-upon rescue club. But it's also lots of fun and competitors come from far and wide to take part in surfing contests, triathlons, cross-country runs, beach sprints, kayak races and inshore rescue boat championships.

(Overleaf) Muriwai Beach, north of Piha, seems to stretch to infinity.